MOOO073014

Parenting Your ADHD Child

Biblical Guidance
for Your Child's Diagnosis

Rita Jamison

New
Growth
Press

newgrowthpress.com

New Growth Press, Greensboro, NC 27404
newgrowthpress.com
Copyright © 2011 by Rita Jamison.
All rights reserved. Published 2011

Cover Design: Tandem Creative, Tom Temple,
tandemcreative.net

Typesetting: Lisa Parnell, lparnell.com

ISBN-10: 1-936768-43-7
ISBN-13: 978-1-936768-43-1

Library of Congress Cataloging-in-Publication Data
Jamison, Rita, 1945–
  Parenting your ADHD child : biblical guidance for your
child's diagnosis / Rita Jamison.
      p. cm.
  Includes bibliographical references and index.
  ISBN-13: 978-1-936768-43-1 (alk. paper)
  ISBN-10: 1-936768-43-7 (alk. paper)
  1. Parents of exceptional children—Religious life. 2. Attention-
deficit hyperactivity disorder—Religious aspects—Christianity.
3. Child rearing—Religious aspects—Christianity. 4. Attention-
deficit-disordered children—Care. 5. Hyperactive children—Care.
I. Title.
  BV4596.P35J36 2011
  248.8'45—dc23
                                              2011038017

Printed in India

28 27 26 25 24 23 22 21   9 10 11 12 13

Attention Deficit Hyperactivity Disorder (ADHD) shows up everywhere. At school, in parking lots, in the grocery store, at Sunday school, during mealtimes, during playtime, with parents, with teachers and with peers—Attention Deficit Hyperactivity Disorder is reportedly the most common label given to children today. The purpose of this minibook is to help parents whose child has received an initial diagnosis of ADHD to think through what that label means and where they need to turn for help.

As a special education public school teacher, a biblical counselor, and someone who works with children individually, I have taught and counseled many children who have been diagnosed with ADHD. As a believer I am persuaded that there is a spiritual component to the issues children with an ADHD diagnosis face. This is because no diagnosis can negate the fact that every human being is made in the image of God. Every child, ADHD or not, has a spiritual nature. Our hearts and our brains are both involved in the choices we make and the ways we think, speak, and act. Even if parents choose to medicate their child there are many other ways they can help their child, as one of God's image bearers, to deal with the behaviors associated with ADHD. I am confident that God's Word offers much wisdom, hope, and comfort for situations like these.

Problems are a part of every child's life. Deuteronomy 6 instructs parents to be continuously teaching and training their children—when they get up in the morning, when they go to bed at night, when they drive somewhere in the van (i.e., when they walk by the way). However, this is not an easy task with an impulsive, easily distracted child. For many parents it is the toughest thing in their lives and something they face every day. God's promise in 2 Peter 1:3 that God's "divine power has given us everything we need for life and godliness through our knowledge of him . . ." is a comfort, but it's also a challenge to figure out exactly how it fits this situation. As a Christian, I decided that if God's Word claims to deal with all of life, that's where I needed to look for answers. This minibook is my attempt to share what I have learned and to help parents see how God's Word does fit this situation.

You Are a Key Part of Helping Your Child

One fundamental thing I've learned is the critical importance of parents. One doesn't have to look far in God's Word to see the role God assigns to parents in bringing up and helping their children. Your perseverance, patience, and love for your child are crucial to help him or her move forward spiritually, socially, and scholastically. It can be especially difficult parenting a child who struggles with the behaviors in the ADHD diagnosis. But God's Word always gives hope. Remember that the promise in 2 Peter 1:3 applies to you as well as your child! God knows you and your child intimately. He will help you do the hard work of faithful parenting as you go to him.

Ask for daily help from the Spirit, and he will hear and answer you with the strength, perseverance, and faith you need as you work with your child. He will pick you up when you fail as a parent, just as he will do for your child. Whether you sin and fail or your child does, you can be confident that God is ready to forgive, restore, and strengthen you to begin again. As Jeremiah wrote in a time of prolonged suffering, "Because of the LORD's great love, we are not consumed, for his compassions never fail. They are new every morning; great is your faithfulness" (Lamentations 3:22–23). In light of the challenge, let me add one more thing: Please don't try to do this alone. Ask friends and family to pray with and for you and your child.

Your Child's Heart Is the Key to Change

A second fundamental truth I've learned is the importance of addressing the heart—that is, the child's thoughts, attitudes, and motives. Matthew 15 explains that our actions come from our hearts. Just as a thorn bush can't produce apples, we cannot expect good behavior to be produced by a bad heart. Just like every other human being, children with an ADHD diagnosis have sinful hearts that need a Savior who "is faithful and just and will forgive us our sins and purify us from all unrighteousness" (1 John 1:9). When children (like their parents) admit their need for forgiveness and trust that Jesus died on the cross to take their punishment, they will be saved. At that point we are promised, "If anyone is in Christ, he is a new creation" (2 Corinthians 5:17). Jesus cleanses us from sin and gives us new hearts that want to please him.

Children who have trusted in Christ as their Savior can be encouraged to make it their goal to please him (2 Corinthians 5:9). Our heavenly Father wants his children to be like his Son (Romans 8:29) and his Holy Spirit commits himself to help bring that about. Young people who understand their new identity and calling have a new motivation to reflect the Lord in their thoughts, words, and actions—and a new hope that they can succeed. This is important because some ADHD characteristics present significant obstacles to obedience. But God has compassion on us in our struggles. Second Corinthians 1:3–4 reminds us that we belong to "the God of all comfort, who comforts us in all our troubles." God doesn't leave us alone in our struggles but loves us, strengthens us, and comforts us in our daily walk with him. As a child learns to trust in the promises of God and believes that God can help him obey, he will be more willing to consider his motives and his actions. Instead of saying, "Johnny, stop doing that," the parent can help a child go deeper and ask, "Johnny, are your thoughts and actions pleasing to Christ right now?"

Even small children can learn to evaluate their motives—what they want—in a particular situation. They need to be taught that they choose their own desires, and wrong desires start the spiral downward to the path of wrong actions. During episodes of misbehavior, children need to learn to ask, "What did I want more than wanting to please God?" Children need to know what behaviors to replace those they are trying to stop.

Many other truths could be mentioned, but the point is that while the following information on specific behaviors of those with ADHD is important, it will only be useful for moms and dads who understand their child's need for a heart changed by Christ. Moms and dads also need to understand the importance of using

God's Word to address the inner person, rather than just outward behaviors.

Understanding ADHD

Now let's look at ADHD specifically. It's been defined by eighteen behavioral characteristics in the Diagnostic and Statistical Manual of Mental Disorders IV TR (hereafter DSM-IV TR).[1]

According to the DSM-IV TR, ADHD is a disturbance of at least six months, during which at least six of eighteen characteristics are present in two different settings (for example, at home and at school). If a child displays at least six of these characteristics at home and at school for six months, that child will be given the label Attention Deficit Hyperactivity Disorder.

I will review the behavioral characteristics as they appear in the DSM-IV TR and discuss biblical truths that could be used with a child exhibiting such behaviors. I think you will be encouraged by the relevance of God's Word to these problems. However, don't be overwhelmed by all the suggestions that follow. There are too many to implement all at once. Pace things for you and your child. Choose one or two ideas and begin to put them into practice. Add others as your child seems ready. Be willing to make adjustments if they don't work well for your family, and seek the counsel of others. As you consider the following suggestions, you will notice that our work with children starts with how God's Word applies to their struggles, and then we set small, relatively attainable goals for each child. You know your child best, so you can use these suggestions as a starting point to help your child live out his faith in the details of his life at home and school.

1. Often fails to give close attention to details or makes careless mistakes in schoolwork, work, or other activities.

Parents who take time to discuss this behavior with their children will often discover wants and desires (James 1:14–15) that led to such behaviors. For instance, the children may have the desire to finish first. Children with this desire often rush through their work. What is the goal here? I must win! In our day there are many children with this as their goal.

Another child (when asked why he rushed through his work) responded, "To get the work over with so I can do something I like." The goal is to have pleasure and ease.

A third reason children rush is because they want to avoid the consequences of not completing the assignment. While there is nothing intrinsically wrong with winning, pleasure, or avoiding consequences, we want our children to have a superior goal—to please God.

I had a child in counseling years ago who was always in a hurry. As a result his papers always looked messy. Sometimes he didn't even bother to erase; he'd just take his pencil and black things out—not just with a single line but with great big black marks. When he did try to erase he wasn't very careful and his paper was ripped and torn, and the presentation of his paper was terrible. Many times others couldn't even find the answers.

His parents brought him to counseling and we shared with him 1 Corinthians 10:31: "Whether you eat or drink or whatever you do, do it all for the glory of God." Then we asked him to evaluate his work using that verse. He said, "Ohhh!" He knew right away that his work did not glorify God. He had to learn that even the smaller details of life can honor God or dishonor him. That's something all children need to learn.

To help this child, we made a simple checklist of four things and asked him to use it on every paper before he turned it in. We instructed him, "When you think you're finished, look at your checklist and make sure your paper is consistent with glorifying God." His teacher helped us by stapling the checklist to every paper he would need to hand in.

Did he like using the list? Not one bit. He often said, "This is good enough. My teacher doesn't care." We would respond, "Is that your goal?" He had to learn to put off the desires of the flesh (what he wanted) and to put on accomplishing his assignments by working at them "with all [his] heart, as working for the Lord" (Colossians 3:23).

2. Often has difficulty sustaining attention in tasks or play activities.

We need to help children who struggle in this area learn to be good stewards of their minds. Paying attention for an extended period of time requires a disciplined mind. The apostle Peter assumed that this takes effort when he talked about "preparing your minds for action" (1 Peter 1:13).

With smaller children, parents may wish to use a kitchen timer to increase attention span. "Last week we worked on the puzzle for three minutes. This week let's try for four minutes." Older children can be instructed about the blessings of paying attention to those whom the Lord has brought into their lives (Proverbs 1:8–9) and the importance of developing the biblical fruit of self-control (Galatians 5:22–23).

When a child is struggling in school, we need to find out what his mind is doing when instruction is being given. Some time ago I worked with a middle school student having trouble in literature class. He was flunking every test he took in literature, yet he was doing great in accelerated math and accelerated science.

The remedial reading principles we worked on did not seem to be of any benefit. One day I finally asked, "What was your mind thinking about when you read that story?"

His response took me by surprise. "My inner tensions," he replied. When I explored this, he talked about unresolved conflicts with adults in his life—including his literature teacher and his parents.

Unresolved conflicts consume our thinking and prevent us from learning. That's all this young man would think about when he was in literature class. He was so frustrated that it carried over to the tutoring room.

We taught him that God wanted him to resolve these conflicts. For him this meant going to his teacher to ask forgiveness for his part of the problem. The next week when he came for tutoring, I could tell by the way he walked that he had asked his teacher for forgiveness. That day in our tutoring session he got 80 percent right. How could he do that? The conflict was resolved and his attention was focused on the reading.

How many times do we allow children to carry conflicts for days thinking they'll get over it? But they don't just "get over it." The problem in another child's life might be bullying or ridicule because his behavior isolates him from other classmates. We need to find out if there are unresolved problems with people and teach children how to solve these problems biblically. Another child might struggle with deep discouragement that academics are so difficult for her. Children need help to resolve these issues too.

3. Often does not seem to listen when spoken to directly.

James instructs believers to "be quick to listen" (James 1:19). Our Lord concluded one of his parables by saying, "Therefore consider carefully how you listen" (Luke 8:18). Proverbs 19:20 instructs, "Listen to advice and accept instruction, and in the end you will be wise." Clearly, learning to listen is important.

Philippians 2:3–4 tells us to "do nothing out of selfish ambition . . . but in humility consider others better than yourselves." When children don't listen, they are doing what they want to do instead of considering others. When they have a task to do, failure to listen is not being responsible. In addition, failure to listen is not giving others the honor they are due (Romans 12:10).

One way to teach children to listen is by asking them to verbally respond each time they are spoken to. When we acknowledge the person who has spoken, it shows them honor and can be the beginning of better listening.

When a child habitually does not listen, make sure you have her attention before you speak to her. Call her name, stand in front of the television, turn off the computer, or do whatever it takes—without yelling. James 1:19–20 says, "Be . . . slow to become angry, for man's anger does not bring about the righteous life that God desires." Yelling will not bring about a righteous life in your child or anyone else.

Be sure your instructions are clear and understandable. Use your fingers to demonstrate how many parts there are to follow. Then ask the child to repeat what you have said. Conclude with "Let me see you do it." It is possible that you need to simplify or shorten your instructions. Your child may not be able to complete more than one task at a time. Paul reminds parents in Ephesians 6:4 not to frustrate their children. Too many complicated instructions might be too difficult for your child. Try fewer and simpler directions as you work with them on their listening.

4. Often does not follow through on instructions and fails to finish schoolwork, chores, or duties in the workplace (not due to oppositional behavior or failure to understand instructions).

The Scriptures have much to say about God's children not only starting well, but also finishing well. Paul instructed the Galatians to "not become weary in doing good, for at the proper time we will reap . . . if we do not give up" (Galatians 6:9). God is committed to helping us complete the work he gives us to do (Ephesians 2:10; Philippians 1:6). When we don't require our children to follow through, we teach them two wrong habits: 1) I don't have to obey; and 2) It's not important to be responsible.

This is a good place to use the principle of cause and effect. As schoolwork, chores, and other duties are assigned, tell the child what will happen if the job gets done and what will happen if it doesn't. Praising and encouraging right behavior, and correcting wrong habits, can help a child persevere and finish well.

5. Often has difficulty organizing tasks and activities.

Boys and girls must be taught that orderliness is a godly characteristic. Scripture says, "Everything should be done in a fitting and orderly way" (1 Corinthians 14:40).

Orderliness requires children to be organized. Any organizational system will help, but organization is something that children must be taught. In addition, someone must oversee it until it becomes a habit. Most organization is drudgery for students, but the result is worth the effort.

For elementary children, parents might choose to buy the child folders for loose papers and a small plastic bucket to store pencils, scissors, crayons, glue sticks, and erasers. Teach the child to use a folder for all loose papers. Label one pocket of the folder "To Do" and the other pocket "Completed." Tell the child, "If the work is not done, keep it on the 'To Do' side. If it is done, put it on the 'Completed' side or turn it in immediately." Tell the child to never put papers in his desk unless they are in a folder or a notebook.

Other forms of organization that have helped students are using lists, prioritizing activities on that list, following a schedule taped on the desk, using a calendar to record due dates, and being told what materials are needed for each task. It also helps children to have a daily routine and, when possible, to have changes in that routine explained before they occur.

6. Often avoids, dislikes, or reluctantly engages in tasks that require sustained mental effort (such as schoolwork or homework).

Some children may be reluctant to engage in required tasks because of a history of failure in that particular activity. Not only are these children frustrated, they may have shut down—quit. These children need much encouragement and assistance from adults to get them going again and to show them that they can be successful.

Aaron was in the third grade when he first entered my special education classroom. My plan was to evaluate what the children remembered after summer break. On this particular day I was checking the students' memory of basic subtraction facts. As I placed a worksheet of subtraction problems on each student's desk, Aaron quickly handed the paper back to me, saying, "I don't do subtraction!"

"You don't do what?" I asked, rather surprised at his response. He matter-of-factly repeated, "I don't do subtraction and my other teacher didn't make me."

I was shocked, to say the least. I put the paper back on Aaron's desk and told him that it was my job to teach him to do subtraction. I explained that I wanted him to do as much as he could by himself, and I would help him with the rest. It was evident that Aaron wasn't happy with my solution. He became red in the face, tore the paper in half, and crossed his arms in stubborn resistance.

"Aaron," I said firmly, "I am here to help you as much as you need, but subtraction is a concept you must learn. You and I together can do the hard things. Hey, I see an easy one on this page. Can you do it while I'm watching you?" He reluctantly did it, and I helped him with a few more.

Then I continued, "You don't have to like subtraction, but you do have to do it! I'm even going to make you good at it by the end of the semester," I quipped. Aaron's reaction was still one of anger and frustration. I could see that he didn't believe me, so I sat down beside him and pointed out the easy problems, one at a time, for him to do on his own.

Each day I sat with Aaron whenever he did subtraction problems, and each day he reacted in anger and repeatedly said, "I don't want to do this! This is hard." For several weeks I encouraged him and insisted that I would help him learn to do them. Our plan was that if Aaron accepted my help, he could go out for recess. He missed recess a few times and then reluctantly began to accept my help with subtraction.

One day, after several weeks, he got a problem completed before I got to him. He was elated! He wanted everyone in the room to see what he had done all by himself. I wasn't surprised that he could do it, but he was!

Students often equate the word *hard* with "impossible," but that isn't true. With our help they can do difficult things. We have to help them understand that it just requires more effort and a determination to think harder.

Children should be encouraged not to give up on hard projects. In my classroom students are not allowed to say "I can't." Those are words we put off, and we put on "I will try" or "Will you help me, please?" God's Word tells us that we "can do everything through him who gives [us] strength" (Philippians 4:13).

7. Often loses things necessary for tasks or activities (e.g., toys, school assignments, pencils, books, or tools).

Children who lose things need to be taught the biblical doctrine of stewardship (1 Corinthians 4:2). God has entrusted them with everything they have, and someday they will stand before him to give an account of how they've handled all they have been given (Romans 14:10). Therefore they need to take care of all that they have. This child may also benefit from learning organizational principles. Everything the child owns should have a place, and everything should be in its place when not in use.

8. Is often easily distracted by extraneous stimuli.

Parents can give their children hope by explaining that as adults they also get sidetracked at times. When people walk into church late, we are all tempted to turn and see who it is, and maybe even let our eyes follow them as they take a seat.

Unlike most adults, children don't know how to direct their attention back to the speaker. Many parents tell their children, "Don't look, don't look." That is not realistic.

Instruct the children, "Take a quick look then get back to your responsibility." Give them a plan—put off an extended gaze and change your thinking to *I can take a quick look, then I must get back to the task* (Ephesians 4:22–24).

9. Is often forgetful in daily activities.

Children who are forgetful in daily activities may need to work on mental priorities. Some "forgetful" children can remember an amazing number of details about their favorite sport's team or television show. When a parent or teacher is speaking, they need to learn to think, *My remembering this information is important to God, so I will make it important to me.* Why is it important to God? Because the person speaking is an authority and children need to listen to authority.

A pocket notepad may help in this situation. Teach children to write down homework assignments, directions, and other important data. This should be signed by the teacher and the parent or the effort will not seem worth it to the student.

It's also helpful to use cause and effect, rather than a "bailout" system. When a kid forgets her gym shoes, she calls her mom, and guess what? Her mom brings her shoes. This is a bailout and children do not learn to be responsible when parents do this.

10. Often fidgets with hands or feet or squirms in seat.

This is a learned habit and new habits can replace it. These children need to be taught to be attentive and to be in control. I tell them, "God made your whole body, so let's use your whole body to listen. Your eyes on the speaker, your ears open, your hands in your lap, and your feet flat on the floor."

Children must be taught to use their eyes, ears, and minds to listen without letting their hands, feet, or thoughts distract them. They need to put off being in motion all the time and put on self-control (Ephesians 4:22–24). Our goal is for the children to be better listeners and to get their work done.

To help one child with this, we devised a plan that whenever I saw him moving around too much, I would walk over to him and tap him on the shoulder. I wouldn't stop teaching; I would merely tap him on the shoulder. That would be his cue to look at himself, find what was out of control, and get it under control.

This child made it a game. When I took one step toward him, he would be in control before I could get there. In a couple weeks he was checking himself on his own. He had learned self-control.

Now, did I have to do it often? At first it seemed about every thirty seconds! It took a great deal of my attention initially. Was it worth it? Yes. Not only did it help the young man grow in self-control, it also benefited the entire class. They were no longer distracted by his behavior and paid attention more easily.

11. Often leaves seat in classroom or in other situations in which remaining seated is expected.

Teach a child to be obedient, even when she doesn't feel like it. John 13:17 tells us that we are happy when we do the things we ought to do. We may not feel like doing it initially, but the feeling will come after we do it.

Teach the child to examine what she wants more than doing what is expected. Does her desire please God?

Whatever plan parents use, they should be sure that the child knows what behavior is to be put off, what change in her thinking needs to be made, and what behavior is to be put on (Ephesians 4:22–24). Then parents should remind the child each morning (in a teaching tone, not an "or else" tone) about the plan and pray with her about it specifically. The parents should tell the child that with God's help, they know she can be successful (Philippians 4:13). Parents also should reassure the child that they will pray for her throughout the day.

As soon as the parents see the child in the evening, they should ask her about her day, praising her accomplishments. Then they should ask her specifically about the problem behaviors. They should try to find out if she was successful for part of the day or if she struggled all day. If she failed they should try to encourage her by reminding her what she should be thinking about during the day.

12. Often runs about or climbs excessively in situations in which it is inappropriate (in adolescents or adults, may be limited to subjective feelings of restlessness).

Parents must prepare their children in advance when they enter a situation where the children will likely run all over the place. Remind the children of the positive and negative consequences of their choices, and give them a consistent put off/put on plan to help them change (Ephesians 4:22–24).

Teach the children the cause-and-effect principle (Galatians 6:7–9). If we sow to our fleshly desires, there are natural consequences that follow. Adults often want to protect children from these consequences, but allowing them to experience some displeasure as a result of their poor choices sometimes helps them learn valuable lessons more quickly.

13. Often has difficulty playing or engaging in leisure activities quietly.

For some children leisure activity means they can do anything they want in any way they want to do it. There is no structure. Providing structure for children in leisure activities promotes safety and security.

A loud child misses instruction, and long periods of missed instructions may result in learning problems. Proverbs 21:23 instructs us that "he who guards his mouth and his tongue keeps himself from calamity." Do the children in our sphere of influence know they can avoid trouble if they keep their mouths and tongues quiet long enough to hear directions?

Teaching the child that she has an outside voice and an inside voice is also helpful. Remind the child which voice she is using and point out whether it is appropriate or not. Then praise or correct the child. I correct children by simply saying to them in an audible whisper, "Say that again." Their voices become softer, and they often use the appropriate voice.

14. Is often "on the go" or acts as if he's "driven by a motor."

First, we need to find out if he acts like he's "driven by a motor" because of frustration.

- Is he failing or succeeding in school?
- Are there unresolved conflicts at home, school, or on the bus?
- Are there conflicts in relationships with friends?
- What other changes are going on in his life? Divorce? Moving?

If we find out what is frustrating the child, we can help him adjust to these things and teach biblical ways to handle problems. In addition, this child needs structure in his life and may find it difficult to maintain it alone. We need to help him by providing reasonable expectations with a routine and schedule. Many families don't have a routine. Children come home from school and things are different from one day to the next. Predictable routines are comfortable for all of us, especially a child who is often on the go.

15. Often talks excessively.

In my experience with children, an excessive talker often talks about others negatively. We can't allow children to tell us negative things about another unless we can help them help the other person. Ephesians 4:29–32 contrasts "unwholesome talk" with building up others. This is a good passage to discuss with your children. God wants us to build others up with our words and tones, but we tend to be condescending and tear others down.

If the person to whom the child is speaking is not part of the problem or the solution, then the child is gossiping. Proverbs 26:20 says that "without wood a fire goes out; without gossip a quarrel dies down." Our job is to help our children be peacemakers and not perpetuate gossips.

16. Often blurts out answers before questions have been completed.

According to Proverbs 18:13, "He who answers before listening—that is his folly and his shame." When children interrupt, it may be due to pride. Some children blurt out answers before a question is finished because they want to show everyone that they know the answer first. Isn't that pride? Humility and putting others first are replacements for pride. Teach children to respect others by listening until others are finished talking.

We also need to help them replace pride by becoming others-oriented. This can be encouraged by children serving alongside their parents. Including children may require extra time to complete a task, and it may seem easier to do it without them, but parents need to include their children in serving opportunities to teach a compassionate and others-oriented attitude.

17. Often has difficulty awaiting turn.

Where would this show up at school? Everywhere! Lining up at the water fountain, in the bathroom, for lunch, for recess, or awaiting other activities. We often hear children arguing about who gets to be first!

This problem stems from selfishness. Again Philippians 2 calls believers to live differently: "In humility consider others better than yourselves. Each of you should look not only to your own interests, but also to the interests of others. Your attitude should be the same as that of Christ Jesus" (vv. 3–5). It is not easy for children to put others first—all of us are naturally selfish! Expect to teach them to share and be concerned about others.

Children need a good, consistent model of putting others first, and parents need to be that model—at home, at church, at the stoplight, and in line at the grocery store. Children learn best what they see practiced.

18. Often interrupts or intrudes on others (e.g., butts into conversations or games).

James 1:19 says that every person should be "quick to listen, slow to speak and slow to become angry."

Teach children to listen without interrupting. Many children display this bad habit because they haven't been taught. Give them a visual or verbal cue to help them change. When a child interrupts me or another child, I say with a gasp, "You're interrupting." That's her cue to put off interrupting and put on listening (Ephesians 4:22–24). It takes time and effort to change bad habits. I use the cue for about four to six weeks before I begin holding a child responsible for a particular sinful habit.

Children need to be instructed to focus on listening rather than what they want to say. They should think,

What I want to contribute is less important than listening to someone else. Parents need to model this by listening carefully when the children speak to them (not multitasking or watching television).

Conclusion

Our culture offers a variety of approaches to deal with ADHD. Often what is missing for both parent and child is the help, encouragement, comfort, power, and wisdom that come from relying on Christ and heeding God's Word. The wisdom of Scripture, applied to a believing heart by a powerful Holy Spirit, can help a child with an ADHD diagnosis change thinking and behavior in ways that honor God and support positive learning and life experiences. Teaching children to consider what God wants them to do and to examine what's going on in their hearts can keep them from simply reacting to their impulses and the distractions around them. When they know that a compassionate God understands their struggles and is willing to help them, it gives children hope and courage to persevere in the change process. It helps their parents persevere too, as they seek to encourage their children to become more like Christ.

Endnote

1. American Psychiatric Association, *Diagnostic and Statistical Manual of Mental Disorders*, 4th Edition Text Revision (Arlington, Va.: APA, 2000).